A CHILD'S ALASKA

CLAIRE RUDOLF MURPHY

PHOTOGRAPHS BY

CHARLES MASON

ALASKA NORTHWEST BOOKS®

ANCHORAGE • PORTLAND

With love to my children, Conor and Megan, in celebration of all our Alaskan memories.
—C.R.M.

The photographs in this book are dedicated to my parents, Janet and Walter Mason.
They bought me my first camera, and offered me what all children need—their
support, encouragement, good humor, and love.
—C.M.

Seventh printing 2003

Library of Congress Cataloging-in-Publication Data
    Murphy, Claire Rudolf.
    A child's Alaska / Claire Rudolf Murphy : photographs by Charles Mason.
    p.   cm.
    Includes bibliographical references.
    ISBN 0-88240-457-1 : (hardbound: alk. paper)
    1. Alaska—Juvenile literature.   2. Alaska—Pictorial works—Juvenile literature.
    [1. Alaska] I. Mason, Charles, 1958–   ill.   II. Title.
F904.3.M87   1994   93-48164
979.8—dc20   CIP
                                                                AC

Managing Editor: Ellen Harkins Wheat
Editor: Susan Ewing
Designer: Elizabeth Watson
Illustrations: Christine Cox
Map: Vikki Leib

Alaska Northwest Books®
An imprint of Graphic Arts Center Publishing Company
P.O. Box 10306, Portland, OR 97296-0306
503-226-2402; www.gacpc.com

Printed in Hong Kong

ALASKA

ARCTIC OCEAN

Barrow

Prudhoe Bay
Kaktovik

SIBERIA

CHUKCHI
SEA

Arctic National
Wildlife Refuge

B R O O K S   R A N G E

ALASKA

ARCTIC CIRCLE

Bering Land
Bridge

Yukon River

Saint Lawrence
Island

Nome

Fairbanks

Yukon River

TRANS-ALASKA PIPELINE

YUKON
TERRITORY

N
W   E
S

BERING
SEA

A L A S K A   R A N G E

Nenana R.

CANADA
USA

0 miles 100
0 km 100

Mt. McKinley

Denali National
Park and Preserve

Tok

Wrangell Mountains

Kuskokwim River

Talkeetna

Bethel

Anchorage
Cook Inlet

Valdez

Cordova

St. Elias Range

Harding
Icefield
Exit Glacier
Seward

Homer

Kenai Fjords
National Park

Mendenhall Glacier

BRITISH
COLUMBIA

Auke Bay   Juneau

GULF OF ALASKA

Petersburg

Kodiak

Ketchikan

Alaska Peninsula

See inset

PACIFIC OCEAN

A l e u t i a n   I s l a n d s

◄ *Alaska is rich in lakes like this one,*
near the Alaska Range. ▲ *Bald eagles thrive*
in the Great Land.

Alaska. Say it slowly and it sounds like a melting glacier or endless miles of treeless tundra. Say it quickly and it sounds like a rushing river or an eagle in flight.

Our forty-ninth state is bigger than Texas, California, and Montana put together. What is it like to grow up in a land with more animals than people? Alaskan children play and go to school like children everywhere. But here their game might be the Eskimo high kick or the classroom might be built on floating timber at a logging camp.

A competitor in the World Eskimo and Indian Olympics toes a sealskin ball in the one-foot high kick. The Olympics, held each year in Fairbanks, feature traditional Native games such as the high kick, stick pull, and greased pole walk.

SNOWSHOE HARE

This homestead family built their own log cabin near Deadfish Lake in the Alaska Interior. Miles from the nearest neighbors, these modern pioneers must be very self-sufficient.

BUSH PLANE

Some children live and go to school in towns or cities like Soldotna, Anchorage, or Fairbanks. Others live in the "bush," in tiny villages, snug harbors, or remote cabins. Children who live in the bush may go to small schools with only one or two teachers, or be home-schooled, taking their lessons at the kitchen table. If you want to visit a friend in the bush, you may have to travel by snowmachine, boat, or small airplane because there probably won't be a road to where you want to go.

A moose cow and calf prune the shrubbery in an Alaskan backyard. During snowy winters, moose often wander into town looking for an easy meal.

RED HUCKLEBERRY

Whether they live in the city or in the bush, young Alaskans might do ordinary things like belong to Scouts, ride bikes, or watch television. But since this is Alaska, children might also stand in their yards and watch green and pink northern lights dance across the evening sky or look out their bedroom windows to see a thousand-pound moose chomp its way through the family garden!

Children in Alaska don't have to go to a national park to see natural wonders. In Juneau, the Mendenhall Glacier, part of an ice field bigger than the state of Rhode

Island, spreads its frozen mass down the mountain just outside town. And in central Alaska, children can look out toward the horizon and point to the tallest mountain in North America. Mount McKinley is known to Alaskans as "Denali," an Athabascan Indian word, which means "The High One." Some children do more than point. Taras Genet, a twelve-year-old boy from Talkeetna, a town near Denali, climbed to the top. So far, he is the youngest person to reach the mountain's summit.

Located in Kenai Fjords National Park, Exit Glacier is part of the 300-square-mile Harding Icefield. Adventurers climb, ski, and hike across these huge areas of snow and ice.

CLIMBING GEAR

Polar bears provide northern Native peoples with meat, fur, and stories to tell. Because its life is tied to the sea, the polar bear is considered a marine mammal along with whales and sea otters.

PANNING FOR GOLD

Some Alaskan children are descendants of the Aleuts, Eskimos, or Indians who migrated across the now-submerged Bering Land Bridge thousands of years ago. Other children are related to European or Russian explorers who sailed to Alaska in search of furs, or to American miners who came looking for gold.

More recently, families may have moved to Alaska to serve at one of the many military bases or to help build the 800-mile-long trans-Alaska pipeline, the longest oil pipeline in the world. Parents in other Alaskan families may work as secretaries, computer operators, teachers, forest rangers, fishermen, gold miners, or bush pilots. And some Alaskan families still live off the land, hunting, trapping, and growing vegetables.

Grizzly bears share their territory with the trans-Alaska pipeline. The pipeline was built above ground wherever construction engineers found permafrost.

Mount McKinley is so massive its slopes give rise to their own clouds. As a result, the peak is often hidden from view. But when the weather is clear, the sight is awesome.

Russia sold Alaska to the United States in 1867 for a little more than seven million dollars—about two cents an acre. Americans back then laughed and called Alaska "Seward's Icebox," after the U.S. secretary of state who was responsible for making the deal.

But today, Alaskan children know their state is a treasure box filled with wonderful wilderness and valuable natural resources such as oil, timber, minerals, and fish. Much

A Denali Park bull caribou rests in the heat of a summer day. The caribou is the only member of the deer family in which both male and female grow antlers.

HOARY MARMOT

of Alaska's land has been set aside as state and national parks like Denali National Park and Preserve, or refuges like the Arctic National Wildlife Refuge.

◀ *Northern lights make colorful magic
in the winter sky.* ▲ *Faces turn frosty when warm breath
meets air that's 50° below.*

Alaska is different from other states
because it sits near the top of the earth. This affects the weather, and
the weather affects what kinds of plants and animals live in a place.
Weather affects the way people live, too. This is why Alaskans sometimes have more in common with their northern neighbors in Canada
and Russia than they do with people in the lower forty-eight states.

Time-lapse photography traces the path of the sun from sunrise to sunset on the shortest day of the year in Fairbanks.

In winter, the earth tilts away from the sun, so the farther north one lives, the colder and darker the winter days. In Barrow, Alaska's northernmost town, the sun doesn't rise above the horizon during December and January, so it's dark all the time except for a couple of hours of twilight every afternoon.

Barrow children draw pictures of the sun and tape them to their classroom windows. But dressed in snowsuits or fur-trimmed parkas and mittens, they play outside anyway, sledding and building snowmen in the moonlight.

Nearly 1,700 miles south of Barrow in Ketchikan, children have almost seven hours of daylight to play in. Alaska is so big that different parts of the state have completely different climates.

▶ *Outhouses are still an important part of rural Alaskan life, and people take pride in their privies.*

▶▶ *Cars creep through Fairbanks ice fog, which forms when air becomes so frigid humidity crystallizes.*

MUKLUKS

In the northern part of the state, temperatures can fall to fifty or sixty degrees below zero Fahrenheit. Wind makes it feel even colder. Bundled up in big boots, fur hats, scarves, and mittens, children are toasty enough at twenty below to walk to the store or feed a yard full of hungry dogs. But at fifty below, most outside play stops because it's hard to breathe and faces can quickly become frostbitten. Cold temperatures send children indoors to read, play basketball, listen to music, or play video games.

School buses and cars need snow tires and special electric heaters to keep engines warm. On the coldest nights, Alaskans plug in their cars so they can be sure the motors will start in the morning.

Totem poles, like this one at Auke Bay, embody the spirit of Southeast Alaska. Southeast's moist, dense forests and rich shores gave birth to strong Indian cultures which still pattern the area's faces and places.

BALD EAGLE

Southern and coastal regions of the state are much milder by Alaskan standards. It may not sound like Miami, but winter temperatures in Anchorage average zero to twenty degrees. Ketchikan and Juneau can be so warm that sometimes rain instead of snow falls from the clouds, sending children sloshing through the streets in tall rubber boots and raincoats.

Mostly though, Alaska winters mean snow. Drifts pushed by the wind may reach to cabin roofs, and in some places of the state the winter's snowfall could bury a car.

Alaskans look forward to the snow because they enjoy skating, ice fishing, snowshoeing, building snow forts, and running sled dogs. At downhill ski slopes and cross-country ski trails around the state, skiers in bright clothes enjoy swooshing through the powdery snow.

Some Alaskans ride their bicycles to school or work year round. Bike lights, reflective tape, and knobby tires make the going safer.

The blanket toss is exciting whether it takes place on the tundra or in a gymnasium. Traditional games like the blanket toss and high kick have been passed down from generation to generation.

Long ago, recreation had specific purposes. Native people created winter games that helped them practice skills they needed for hunting. In the Eskimo blanket toss, for instance, a person climbs onto a big blanket held around the edges by many people and is thrown high into the air to spot caribou, whales, and other animals far off in the distance. Originally, the blanket was made from the skin of a female walrus. Today,

WALRUS

This Athabascan man wears elegant hand-beaded moccasins. Traditional Native arts and crafts are a vital part of today's Alaska.

▶▶ A musher crosses glare ice on the Yukon River in the 1,000-mile-long Yukon Quest Sled Dog Race.

Native Alaskan children and adults spend hours practicing this and other games such as the one-foot high kick so they can participate in events like the annual World Eskimo and Indian Olympics.

The tradition of sewing skins into useful items like blankets, fur-trimmed parkas, and mukluks is carried on even today. Alaskan Native peoples still practice skin sewing and other traditional crafts including basket weaving, ivory carving, beadwork, and mask making. Many elders pass these crafts on to their grandchildren or visit schools to teach the skills to students. Young people smile as they struggle to thread needles or carve wood with a knife.

◄ *Even in the summer, Arctic Ocean ice
may not melt away completely.* ▲ *Strong bonds
develop between sled dogs and humans.*

When spring comes to Alaska, days get longer and snow begins to melt. The first time the sun rises above the horizon in Barrow, children greet it with songs. Dogsledders and snowmachiners, who have driven on frozen rivers all winter long, listen for the crash, boom, and tinkle of "breakup," when river ice breaks into chunks and starts moving slowly downstream. Alaskans gather on the riverbanks to celebrate this sign of spring.

Dall sheep are creatures of northern high country. The unique white sheep is similar to the Rocky Mountain bighorn, but the two are different species.

Flowers sprout as the days get longer. King salmon swim in from the sea and push themselves up the rivers to spawn. Dall sheep and mountain goats give birth to their young and shed their shaggy winter coats. Sandhill cranes, geese, and songbirds that have wintered as far away as South America, Africa, and the Antarctic return to Alaska to nest. Their calling and honking overhead is a joyful sign that summer is on its way.

Eager young people trade ice skates, sleds, and snowmachines for in-line skates, bikes, and four-wheelers. Teenagers don't waste any time, and start to wear shorts as soon as the snow melts. Softball players oil their gloves and wait for muddy fields to dry out. Children of fishing families mend nets, sharpen hooks, and get ready for the fishing season.

Even a July bike ride can be chilly when you live in the Arctic. Today this Kaktovik boy wears a summer parka, but tomorrow may be warm enough for a T-shirt.

TUFTED PUFFIN

*◄ The midnight sun entices vegetables
to grow huge. ▲ Eskimo boys at Scout camp
enjoy a summer plunge.*

D uring the summer the earth tilts toward the sun, so the farther north one lives the more sunlight there is. In Barrow, the sun never dips below the horizon during May, June, and July. Throughout the state, summer temperatures average in the sixties, but can occasionally reach into the nineties in some places like Fairbanks. On the hottest days, swimmers dive into still-chilly lakes and rivers for a quick dip, ignoring their goosebumps.

31

White-water rafters on the Nenana River hope for thrills and chills with no spills. Recreation on Alaska's many rivers is a major summer pastime.

Summer-happy Alaskans grab the mosquito repellent and kiss cabin fever goodbye. They float rivers, go camping and fishing, play baseball, and hike. With the long hours of daylight, gardeners grow giant vegetables that they will enter in fairs around the state. Now, instead of snow, the land is covered with lush green leaves, bright-magenta fireweed, and Alaska's state flower, the tiny blue forget-me-not.

The halibut caught on this charter sport fishing trip out of Homer weighed between 30 and 100 pounds. The largest halibut on record weighed 495 pounds and was caught near Petersburg.

KING CRAB

On the ocean, young and old fishermen catch salmon, halibut, shrimp, herring, and crab. On beaches and riverbanks, Native families work in the same fish camps their ancestors have used for hundreds of years. Night and day they work catching, cleaning, and drying salmon for the winter, barely taking time to sleep in the tents. Sometimes the children help and sometimes they run off to play with cousins, brothers, and sisters.

◄ A red fox carries off a hare dinner.
*▲ Blueberries and cranberries will be a treat
in this girl's pancakes.*

As summer gives way to fall, animals, birds, and berry pickers have harvested most of the wild blueberries, but cranberries and rosehips are just getting ripe. Children attach bells to their berry pails to warn away bears, who also love berries. Alaskan autumns are beautiful but brief. Animals and people notice the days getting shorter and use the season to prepare for winter.

Ptarmigan remain in Alaska all winter, foraging under snow for twigs and buds.

▸ *The musk ox's underfur, called* qiviut, *is collected and spun into one of the world's rarest and warmest fibers.*

Caribou, moose, musk oxen, and sled dogs grow thicker coats. Ptarmigan, arctic foxes, and snowshoe hares trade their brown feathers or fur for white—perfect camouflage when the snow flies. Many birds migrate south. Grizzly bears and ground squirrels fatten themselves before the long winter's sleep of hibernation.

Gardeners pick the last of their broccoli and cabbage before the first frost, and children go with their parents to hunt caribou and moose.

School begins and students replace fishing poles and baseball bats with books and backpacks. Ice forms on rivers and coasts. As the nights get colder, children dig to the bottoms of closets to find snow boots and coats, gloves and hats. Soon, it is winter again.

In 1988 three gray whales were late beginning their migration south and became trapped in the closing polar ice near Barrow.

▶▶ Villagers and other volunteers cut a mile-long string of breathing holes to help the whales get to open water.

GRAY WHALE FEEDING ON THE OCEAN'S BOTTOM

◀ *A polar bear mother and her two cubs travel across pack ice.*
▲ *Siberian Yupik women from Russia and Alaska share a dance.*

So what is it like to be a child in Alaska? It's dogsledding under the northern lights and fishing under the midnight sun. It's school and river trips, moose and mosquitoes, eagles and airplanes.

Alaska. Say it slowly and it sounds like people and animals circling together through the seasons. Say it quickly and it sounds like children laughing in this Great Land.

Alaska!

GLOSSARY

ALASKA

Our largest state. The name comes from the Aleut word Alyeska (al-YES-ka) meaning "The Great Land." Only half a million people live in Alaska, which became our forty-ninth state in 1959.

ALASKA NATIVE

Descendants of one of three groups of peoples—Aleut, Eskimo, and Indian—who migrated to Alaska from Asia thousands of years ago over the Bering Land Bridge. Many Alaska Natives still hunt and fish as a way of life and carry on artistic traditions such as beadwork, skin sewing, and carving. Native peoples make up about twenty percent of Alaska's population. (See Aleut, Eskimo, and Indian.)

ALEUT (AL-ee-oot)

One of three groups of Alaska Native peoples. Aleuts settled on the Alaska Peninsula and Aleutian Chain of islands.

BERING LAND BRIDGE

An ancient migration route that people and animals followed from Asia to North America. This route was flooded over when the Ice Age ended and the sea rose.

BUSH

A word used to describe remote Alaska locations not served by roads.

◄*This "Two-Headed Moose of Denali" is actually a cow and calf looking both ways while they cross the road.*

▲ *An Inupiat Boy Scout warms up after a swim.*

NOOTKA ROSE

Many Alaskan bush pilots fly floatplanes so they can land on lakes, rivers, or shorelines. In the winter, floats may be replaced with skis.

CABIN FEVER
A feeling of restlessness when people must stay inside because it's too cold outdoors.

ESKIMO
One of three groups of Alaska Native people. Two different subgroups of Eskimo live in Alaska, each with its own language: the Inupiat (in-OOP-ee-at) who settled along the Arctic Ocean and Chukchi (CHUK-chee) Sea and the Central Yup'ik (YOOP-ik) who settled along western Alaska rivers and the Bering Sea. Another subgroup of Yupik people, the Siberian Yupik, speak yet another language and live on Alaska's Saint Lawrence Island and in Russia.

FISH CAMP

A traditional spot where families spend the summer catching and preserving fish for the winter.

GLACIER

A large, long-lasting field of ice that forms when more snow falls than melts.

HIBERNATION

A sleeplike state in which some animals pass the winter. Animals hibernate in a den or in some other protected place.

HIGH KICK

Traditional Native game that tests agility and balance. In the one-foot high kick, the contestant hops, kicks one foot up to touch a sealskin ball, and lands on the same foot without falling. There is also a two-foot high kick.

INDIAN

One of three groups of Alaska Native people. Athabascan (ath-uh-BASK-uhn) Indians settled from the Brooks Range to the Canadian border, along Cook Inlet, and at Cordova. There are eleven distinct Athabascan languages. Three Pacific Northwest Coast Indian groups—Haida (HI-duh), Tlingit (CLINK-it), and Tsimshian (shim-shee-ANN)—settled in Southeast Alaska.

LOGGING CAMP

A temporary settlement, sometimes built on

SILVER SALMON

floats, where loggers and their families live while working in the woods.

LOWER 48

The connected forty-eight states in the continental United States.

MIDNIGHT SUN

A term used for the summer sun, which stays above the horizon for long hours in the middle of the night.

MOUNT McKINLEY (Denali)

The tallest mountain in North America, at 20,320 feet. In 1980, Mount McKinley National Park was expanded to six million acres and its name changed to Denali National Park and Preserve.

MUKLUKS

Warm boots traditionally worn by Eskimos and other northern residents. Mukluks are often knee-high and made from the skins of animals such as seals or caribou. Mukluks may also be made of canvas or other material.

NORTHERN LIGHTS (aurora borealis)

Shimmering bands of light that sometimes appear in northern skies during hours of darkness. The dancing streaks of green, blue, white, red, and purple are caused by charged particles energized by the sun. Early northern

Other mountains outside North America may peak at higher elevations, but in terms of pure height from base to top, Denali is the tallest mountain in the world.

cultures thought the lights came from the spirits of animals, or children who had died at birth.

PERMAFROST
A layer of soil beneath the ground's surface that remains frozen year round.

PTARMIGAN (TAR-muh-gun)
A grouse-like bird with feathered feet. The willow ptarmigan is Alaska's state bird.

QIVIUT (KIH-vee-oot)
The soft undercoat of a musk ox, which is spun into yarn and used to knit hats and scarves.

SNOWMACHINE
The word Alaskans use for snowmobile.

SPAWN
To deposit and fertilize eggs. Most salmon spawn in the gravel of riverbeds.

TOTEM POLES
Cedar logs carved and painted to represent legends and special creatures. Pacific Northwest Coast Indians are well known for their totem poles, which stand up to eighty feet tall.

TUNDRA
The relatively flat, treeless plain found in arctic regions. Permafrost keeps trees from growing, but low-lying plants such as lichens, moss, and small wildflowers thrive. Caribou, musk oxen, birds, foxes, bears, and other kinds of wildlife also live on the tundra.

TLINGIT TOTEM POLE